A Global Approach to Equitable Internet Access

By

Michael Andrew Lambert Jr

Table of Contents

Abstract	5
Introduction	9
Literature Review	13
Proposed Solution	33
Conclusion	51
References	55
Appendix A	75
Appendix B	69
Appendix C	73

Abstract

This paper focuses on the current state of the internet on a global scale, and how different internet access is in various countries and regions, and how a third of our global population still does not have access to the internet. In developed countries we often have an abundant access to internet, but in developing countries they may not even have internet at all. This paper goes further and discusses the impact that internet has on education, the economy and global inclusion—it has a direct impact to how we learn, how we interact and how we work together. After acknowledging the current state of our global internet infrastructure, this paper dissects various solutions as to how we can further improve both developed and developing countries internet infrastructure. Proposed solutions include to further develop existing internet infrastructure as well as build non existence infrastructure to area without internet access, examples of such are provided by public-private partnerships (such as Google's Project Loon and Meta's Free Basics) which will make internet more accessible through subsidies. Furthermore while building adequate internet infrastructure, if owning a computer is financially unobtainable for individuals and families in the area, focus on building community access points such as libraries and Telecentres. Lastly by enforcing open internet policies, it will preserve an equitable internet for all across the globe. The following paper takes a deep dive in advocating for a fair and open internet.

Introduction

In this modern era where the internet is seemingly a part of our everyday lives, as we use it in education and the workplace, it drives our economy. However on a global scale, an individual's experience with the internet can vary drastically. Despite how far technological advancements have come over the last couple decades, there is significant gap in internet access between high-income developed countries and regions, and low-income developing countries and regions. In the early days of the internet, the internet was a luxurious resource only available to universities and the government and has developed into to a more accessible utility and commodity (Elon University n.d.), and has become essential to access education, healthcare, and other economic opportunities. This paper dives into the complex nature of internet access throughout the globe, where we take a look at culture diversity and consider the ethical implications. Per example, Alvarez and Diez (2023) argue that access to the internet is a fundamental basic human right as Mexico's Supreme Court has decided, in contrast to Hoang's (2021) study where the censorship of China's Great Firewall [GFW] challenge this verdict. To bridge evident disparities we need to take a close look at where we currently stand policy and technological wise (to discover what we can and need to do) to make technological, ethical, and political changes with a global scope to improve internet access.

Literature Review: Globalization of the Internet

Introduction of Literature Review

In today's digital world, the internet is a crucial tool that has become a part of our everyday lives. The internet is deep seeded within our social life, goes hand in hand with our economy and stretches past our political borders into international landscapes. This review takes a deep look into various scholarly sources to discover the diversity of how people across the globe access the internet. In developed countries it is quite easy to take the internet for granted, however in under developed countries and regions access to the internet is a vastly different experience. Not only do we take a look at the economic and technological barriers, but we also dive into the questionable ethics, in countries like Mexico the Supreme Court have decided that the internet is a human right (Alvarez, 2023), while in other countries such as China, censor their citizens access to the internet (Hoang, 2021). The following literary review will dive into these contrasting points, in which we will see what can be done to further progress internet globalization.

Is the Internet a Human Right?

Alvarez and Diez (2023) are advocating that the internet is fundamentally a basic human right, in which the internet plays a crucial role in self expression, education and access to information. Alvarez and Diez (2023) teach the 'four A's' methodology—Availability, Accessibility, Acceptability, Adaptability. They draw attention to Mexico's Supreme Court decision as landmark case, in which the court's verdict is that the Internet is a basic human right. Alvarez and Diez (2023) argue that the internet is not only a fundamental human right, but also plays a pivotal role in enhancing social cultures, democracy and the economy. Furthermore, Alvarez and Diez (2023) insists that we have an ethical obligation to ensure everyone universally has the right to access the internet as well as information. This is a stark contrast to how the general populous are able—allowed—to access the internet on different parts of the globe. Per example, Hoang (2021) goes into great detail on how China has what is called The Great Firewall, which highly censors how their citizens access and interact with the internet.

In contrast, Hoang (2021) sheds light on China's Great Firewall, which restricts their citizens from accessing information and infringes on 'online freedoms'. Hoang's research reveals an overbearing amount of censorship through DNS filtering, aimed at controlling their nation's online discourse and limiting access to international insight (Hoang, 2021). This diverse governance on the internet is a vastly different from what Alvarez and Diez (2023) discussed of how the internet is not only a human right but it also needs to be Acceptable and Adaptable—an open fair internet. The polarizing policies these two countries have over the internet emphasizes the need to take a closer look if the internet should be generally considered a human right on a global scale, or if China is correct in censoring their internet.

Alvarez and Diez (2023) and Hoang (2021) bring attention to the how different the internet is handled ethically across the globe and open that discussion on internet rights. While Alvarez and Diez (2023) take a headstrong approach with their 'four A's' methodology and stance that the internet is basic human right, Hoang (2021) study on the Great Firewall show the difficulties in balancing balancing individual freedoms and protecting national security. Together Hoang and Alvarez and Diez strengthen our understanding of the governance over the internet globally. This comparison beckons the question if the internet should universally be considers a basic human right or if censorship, like in China, is justifiable.

Educational and Societal Relevance

Bradshaw (2018) explores internet accessibility and how it's role curates international education, putting focus on how the internet bridges cultural barriers and cultivates global understanding. The article discusses barriers to internet adoption that are still prevalent today, mainly in developing countries and regions where technological advancements remain physically and economically challenging. Bradshaw highlights the ethical need to bring internet access for educational purposes, which can be done by incorporating inclusive policies. Recent statistics showcase that roughly 2.6 billion people—our roughly one-third of the world's population—still lack reliable internet remain offline, the majority of them being low income countries and regions (International Telecommunication Union, 2023).

Bradshaw's (2018) analysis can be further supported by the findings of Alvarez and Diez (2023), whom argue that the internet should be classified as a basic human right. As mentioned earlier, Alvarez and Diez (2023) methodology of the 'four A's'—Availability, Accessibility, Acceptability and Adaptability—highlight the importance of cultural inclusiveness, as this method not only focuses on the physical and technical aspects of internet access but also focuses on the content with an open and fair internet. This goes hand in hand with receiving education globally through access to the internet. For example, UNESCO report (2023) highlights that access to online educational resources can directly impart educational outcomes. However socioeconomic barriers in developing countries is one of the biggest hurdles in achieving this goal. Bradshaw (2018) and Alvarez and Diez (2023) bring the focal point to how accessible internet can empower us both economically and educationally, while highlighting ethical constraints in regards to the equality and inclusiveness diversity of globally gaining access to the internet.

The Infrastructure and Economic Impact of the Internet

Dao (2017) goes into great detail and analysis of the internet usage across the globe, diving into the diversiting across countries and highlighting their infrastructures, the affordability and technological advancements. The study reveals the contrast in internet access between developed and developing countries. For example, over 90% of the population of high income countries/regions have reliable internet access, only roughly 30% of people in low income countries/regions have internet access (World Bank, 2024). This drastic gap between developed and developing countries, highlights the need for access points such as libraries, to bridge the gap for areas that lack internet access. For low income countries, owning a computer is the main barrier to having internet access so having public computers is an ethical necessity. According to a report by International Telecommunication Union (2023), the average cost to purchase a base laptop in low income counties was roughly $500, which coincidentally is more than twice the amount of the relative monthly income. Whereas in lower middle income countries, the quality and cost become more of a concern. For example, the average internet speed in lower middle income countries is about 40% slower when compared to high income countries, and the average cost of a broadband internet service can cost as much as 10% of their monthly income—in lower middle income regions (International Telecommunication Union, 2024).

As Alvarez and Diez (2023) touched based on having a quality internet access directly affects education, which highlights the necessity for decent technological infrastructure, which will shorten the diverse gaps across varying countries. Alvarez and Diez (2023) have a mutual outlook as Dao (2017) as it is important to improve internet quality and cost, especially in developing countries. Both Dao (2017) and ALvarez and Diez(2023), highlight the necessity for improving internet infrastructure, which can promote economic growth and reduce global inequalities. By improving internet access globally, we can work towards a more equal world.

The Governance of the Internet and International Trade

Gnangnon (2022) discusses how access to the internet impacts international trade, and the studies find that there is a heavy correlation between an open fair internet and economic stability. The study showcases how countries with a more openness to their internet access tend to generate a stable tax revenue within their country, demonstrated by how an increased access to the internet creates fluid business operations, enhances accounting and seamlessly integrates with international business deals. Specifically, Gnangnon's (2022) study shows that countries that exhibit higher amounts of freedom when it comes to internet access tend to have a stabler tax revenue system with higher revenues due to a transparent—non-censored—internet as well as efficiency in the market due to all of the former. This highlights an ethical point while we create policies for internet governance, we must take into consideration to incorporate open trade and digital inclusiveness for economic stability across borders.

To compliment Gnangnon's findings, Alvarez and Diez (2023) argue the importance of digital equality, in which equal internet access isn't just technological barrier but also a critical component to ensure a fair global economy. They argue that unequal internet access can create drastic gaps in the global economy, noted in the differences between high income and low income—developed and developing—countries. Limited internet access in developing and poorer countries prevent the population from fairly engaging in international trade and education. Gnangnon (2022) and Alvarez and Diez (2023) together demonstrate how access and quality to the internet plays vital role impacting our global economy. These findings call for ethical considerations while establishing policies for internet governance, that support economic stability across international borders.

Legal Challenges on a Global Scale

Tiburcio and Albuquerque (2023) take on a deep analysis of the legal challenges and complexities around governance of the internet, putting the focal point on the jurisdiction conflicts on the borderless internet. Their studies highlight the challenges that courts endure worldwide while applying traditional national (bordered/ territorial) policies to the global nature of the internet. The challenges that arise are the difficulty in determining which country's current laws are applicable to internet based activities, the proper method and/or procedure to handle internet conflicts that cross international borders (such as, if content was created in Spain but accessed in Argentia, who is legally responsible?) and how to manage such conflicts that arise between two countries that govern the internet differently (Mexico vs China).

Tiburcio and Albuquerque (2023) discuss the hurdles of applying traditional jurisdiction to internet related disputes, the fact that content from the internet can simultaneously be accessed globally past national border—and viceversa—complicates the situation. For example, if created content the beckons a legal suit such as defamation is posted in one country, but accessed in another, deciding which countries laws should apply to this situation is problematic. This is showcased in court rulings from Brazil, Europe and North America, each had to establish a verdict and overcome these challenging concepts, each addressing this concepts in a semi-similar fashion.

The courts in Brazil focus on if the content is accessed within national borders. Brazilian authorities care more about internet content within their local jurisdiction, and the local impacts. For example, Brazilian Superior Court of Justice ruled that if internet content (website) is accessible within Brazil, it may be subject to local jurisdiction, despite if the servers hosting the website is overseas (Tiburcio and Albuquerque, 2023). In the United States, the case of Zippo Manufacturing Co. v Zippo Dot Com, Inc. showcased the importance of intention to determine jurisdiction, the framework. The "Zippo Sliding Scale" (Jennings, 2005) developed in this case categorizes and judges websites/web-content based on their commercial nature and degree of interactivity, which will determine whether or not the legal justification is applicable in the current state. The idea behind the "Zippo Sliding Scale" and the verdict of this case is that, if a a website's business operations involve people and/or making money in said state—than that states laws and courts should be applicable. This is explicit in the ruling: "When a defendant makes a conscious choice to conduct business with the residents of a forum state, 'it has clear notice that it is subject to suit there.' ... Dot Com was under no obligation to sell its services to Pennsylvania residents. It freely chose to do so, presumably in order to profit from those transactions" (Zippo Manufacturing Co. v. Zippo Dot Com, Inc., 1997).

The European Court of Justice on the other hand uses a "mosaic" method, which allows multiple jurisdictions based on where the content was accessed as well as the intentions and interests of the parties involved. The ethical dilemmas that are situated in the line between global internet freedoms and local policies and regulations. The difficulty in regulating this because apparent when countries govern the internet differently, each whom approach freedom of expression, individual rights and economically uniquely. Tiburcio and Albuquerque (2023) highlight that as the local laws in vary between countries, lead to conflict of disputes when handling crossborder internet cases.

The stark contract becomes apparent when we compare Mexico's Supreme Court decision that the internet is a human right (Alvarez, 2023) while China's access to the internet is highly censored due to China's Great Firewall (Hoang, 2021). With a highly sanitized and censored internet, it is apparent that the governance over the internet becomes quite manageable, the tradeoff with this approach is the sacrifice of our basic human rights. Tiburcio and Albuquerque (2023) further discuss on approaches some international law take on governance over the internet, such as consideration to where the defendant lives and where is the location of damages. Tiburcio and Albuquerque (2023) go into great detail regarding facts, court cases and examples on how difficult it is to govern the internet past international borders.

Summary of Literature Review

This literature review highlights the vast and difficult arena of the global internet. It takes into consideration and beckons the question if the internet is/ should be considered a basic human right. Bradshaw (2018) and Alvarez and Diez (2023) dually highlight that internet accessibility and internet quality have a direct impact on education, economic growth and societal growth. Their studies showcase that providing accessible internet can bridge cultural gaps between countries and foster a global understanding, with shedding light to the socioeconomic barriers in developing countries. Dao (2017) showcases how important it is to bring infrastructure and economies into consideration, stating that with improved internet access we can build towards diminishing global inequalities and advocate for global economic growth and stability. Tiburcio and Albuquerque (2023) discuss the legal difficulties governing the internet passed international borders—borderless internet—We take a deep dive into how we should govern the internet, just how complex and difficult it becomes on a global scale. Lastly, further research is likely needed to establish and formulate a proper plan to address the legal complexities of this topic.

Proposed Solution: Global Internet Access Initiative

Introduction of my Proposed Solution

Addressing the global disparities surrounding internet access, we need to reach a point of singularity with the internet, a solution that is both ethical and addresses the global incqualities—regardless of location, culture and socioeconomic status. The solution to this problem needs to shorten and bridge the gap between developed and developing countries/regions to build global economic stability, foster educational opportunities, and mandate internet access as a fundamental and basic human right.

Equal Internet Access

To achieve equal internet access globally isn't an easy task and requires much care and consideration. Which includes developing the proper infrastructure, regulating and reforming current regulatory policies, and to establish/ extend community access points—such as libraries.

Infrastructure Development

Public-Private Partnerships:

Public-private partnerships [or PPPs]—collaborative agreements between governments and private corporations—are a key asset to improve internet access in developing countries (World Bank, 2024). At the intersection of technical expertise and funding from private corporations and the public focus from government agencies, PPPs are a crucial part to bring a globally equal internet. A notable example of a PPP is Google's Project Loon, which is a project that disperses high altitude atmospheric balloons to provide internet access to remote and secluded regions (Katikala, 2014). This project has helped bring relief to regions suffering from natural disasters, Google's Project Loon was deployed to bring internet to Puerto Rico after the devastating aftermath of Hurricane Maria, thus restoring and/or mitigating internet connectivity where traditional internet sources have been damaged or demolished entirely (Nieva, 2017). Facebook —now Meta— had it's own PPP program called Internet.org—later got renamed to Free Basics—is another program with the intent of brining internet to developing and under developed countries and regions such as India and Kenya (Nothias, 2020). Both Google's Project Loon and Meta's Free Basics are two examples where big tech companies have already pursued and implemented various projects to help build a global internet.

Affordable Internet and Technologies:

If we provide financial support—or subsidize the cost—of internet based devices we can help bring the technologies to low income countries and regions. This can be funded by government grants, various subsidies and partnerships with manufacturers—Google and Meta already have been involved, maybe petition Samsung, Apple, Microsoft, etc—to reduce and/or offset the cost of devices such as laptops and smartphones. One example is the "One Laptop per Child" (OLPC) program, the entire basis is to bring affordable and sustainable laptops to children in developing countries, so that children growing up in low income developing countries and regions would have access to current technology and in turn engage in a proper education (Kraemer, 2009). The OLPC program is a proven example on how affordable technology has a direct and positive impact on education and global connectivity, which beckons the need for more programs like this one. Lastly, GIZ has a "Digital Inclusion" program situated in various African countries, which brings low cost smartphones to developing and low income areas. This program has given these areas access to the internet, when otherwise they wouldn't have the opportunity to engage in international trade, literacy and education (GIZ, 2020). If we can petition more companies to partake and build these ethical programs, we can globally reach new heights through an open and equal internet.

Additional Access to The Internet:

Public internet has been life changing for many even in developed countries and regions, for those who could otherwise not afford the device or internet service, examples of public internet access points are internet cafes and public libraries. These locations offer free to low cost internet service and can serve as crucial hubs to apply for jobs, turn in assignments, and engage in the economy in other aspects. The 'Telecentre' model, demonstrates this approach, Telecentres are centers located within local communities to provide internet access and computer training (International Telecommunication Union, 2000).

Theses centers have been implemented in the rural areas of Bangladesh, and have greatly improved digital literacy and access to educational resources, highlighting the need to build more community based access points similar to these Telecentres. Lastly, the "Internet for All" program— by International Telecommunication Union (ITU)—aims to bring internet to rural and underserved areas by building and implementing internet access points. This program's goal isn't just to bring internet connectivity but to also be locations for digital skills training which will also build local economies (International Telecommunication Union, 2021).

Policy and Regulations

Universal Service Funds (USFs):

Universal Service Funds is a fund, typically set up and managed by local governments and is used in the

United States, to be dispursed to make sure individuals can access basic telephone and internet services. USFs are typically funded with contributions from telephone companies. From there funds are then dispersed to support and build infrastructure projects in low income areas (Dorward, 2013). For example, the Federal Communications Commission (FCC)—in the United States—oversees the Universal Service Fund to provide internet access in rural and low income areas. These USFs have been proven effective in diminishing the gap between access to the internet and lack there of (International Telecommunication Union, 2023). The idea of USFs can be adapted and used on a global scale to remedy the economic inequalities with having internet access. While Alvarez and Diez (2023) do not mention USFs specifically, however they argue how important infrastructure investments are to improve access to digital devices and the internet, which could be supported through USFs. By establishing global scale USFs we can ensure that internet access is possible in low income and rural areas.

Open Internet Policies:

Open internet policies and regulations—sometimes known as net neutrality—are an essential part of maintaining access to a fair and equal internet, including content and services. These regulations are in place to prevent Internet Service Providers (ISPs) from censoring and providing a bias internet experience—such as only displaying specific content, apps, and/or services. These regulations ensure that all users have a fair experience with an equal access to online resources, regardless of their location and/or economic status (American Library Association, 2024).

Enforcing net neutrality is crucial to advocate for an open, fair and accessible internet. For example, the 'Open

Internet Rule' by the Federal Communications Commision —FCC—established in 2015 was an important act to enforce net neutrality in the United States. It's goal was aimed to prevent ISPs from throttling, censoring and blocking legal content and applications (Federal Communications Commission, 2015). The whole concept of net neutrality is important—and crucial—to be implemented as to prevent internet censorship. Tiburcio and Albuquerque (2023) have argued and advocated for the importance of regulations that support open and fair internet, while addressing the legal challenges we still face when regulating content that crosses international borders.

Universal Service Funds (USFs) and open internet regulations are important aspects to consider and implement to achieve a global equal internet. USFs, that are funded by telephone companies, are built to provide adequate internet infrastructure to underdeveloped areas, which addresses the financial barrier for providing equal access to the internet. USFs and open internet regulations are a crucial part of advancing towards having a global equal access to the internet.

Governing the Internet Ethically

Governing the internet effectively is critical to maintain an open and fair internet. This requires that we focus on collaborating internationally with transparency and accountability. By working together, we can ensure that an open and fair internet remain accessible to all.

Collaborating Internationally:

A global scale regulatory framework is critical to be able to address and administer the open internet, while being cognitive and empathetic towards cultural diversity, we can unsure the internet is a universal human right around the globe. The oversight for these policies and regulations should be conducted by international organizations such as the United Nations— this would ensure ethical internet use, protection of data and protection on digital rights. Furthermore, formulating clear transparent guidelines for internet activities that cross international borders would address legal disputes, taking it further by creating an international organization. This international organization would specifically address data privacy, data piracy, cyber crimes, and intellectual property infringement & protection. By doing so, this would create a streamline and transparent path for legal resolutions, which would support a fair and open internet experience across the globe and various jurisdictions.

Transparency and Accountability:

Transparency reports play a vital role for advocating and promoting accountability as well as building trust. Mandating that Internet Service Providers (ISP) and relevant tech companies publish timely reports that detail how they handle data, privacy and government requests for information will ensure that all participants are held accountable. These reports should include detailed numeric insights into the depths of how companies manage their data, and how they respond to and address privacy concerns —building public trust. More-so, by developing an ethical set of standards—for data usage and collection—we can protect individual privacy and mitigate the mishandling of data.

Together these—international collaboration, a standard of ethics and transparency/accountability—are fundamental aspects to achieve effective oversight and governance towards an global open, fair and equal internet.

Educational Opportunities and Programs

To maximize the potential benefits of having accessible internet, we need to incorporate quality educational programs that will improve digital skills and foster an online learning environment.

Digital Literacy Programs:

By providing digital literacy classes as part of schools main curriculums, that would teach students valuable skills such as online research, cybersecurity, digital/data privacy, digital responsibility and how to communicate in a digital space. By incorporating these studies into school systems, students will be well prepared to participate in the digital world safely, responsibly and efficiently (Bradshaw, 2018). Furthermore, organize and provide workshops and classes that will provide training sessions for students and adults alike in low income and developing regions, this will enhance their skillsets, improve employability and greatly improve their overall quality of life. The lessons within these workshops and classes will cover basic computer skills, internet safety and online job searching—including resume building and learning additional skills. Programs such as these ensure that today's current population and forthcoming generations are equipped to engage in the modern job market.

Online Educational Resources:

Open Educational Resources (OER) are sources that are freely accessible to anyone with open licensing, a simple example of this would be the resource within a public library. These OERs can provide high quality content to students across the globe. Organizations such as UNESCO (2023) play a crucial role in providing these resources, and ensuring that education remains accessible regardless of any economical or geographical barriers. Furthermore, partnerships with colleges and other educational institutions and platforms like Coursera,

Udemy and Khan Academy can offer free to low cost online courses to individuals facing economic barriers. These Massive Open Online Courses (MOOCS) provide knowledge and learning opportunities to a wide range of subjects, making education accessible to all. An example of these Partnerships is with the Denver Public Library, anyone may freely sign up for a Library Card which grants the individual full access to Udemy courses (Denver Public Library, n.d.). These collaborative programs and courses can provide a vast array of knowledge and opportunity—from fundamental literacy to advanced technical skills. By providing collaborative educational environments such as those, greatly enhances educational opportunities across the globe that directly impacts our global economy.

Concluding the Solution

Achieving a fair and ethical accessible internet worldwide needs a thorough strategy that includes infrastructure to be built, governance with policies to be reformed, educational programs and economic tools. By learning from these scholarly resources we can incorporate a plan to build towards an open and free internet worldwide.

Conclusion

In conclusion, the gap in internet access across the globe is a major issue that impacts educational opportunities, stunts economic growth, and hinders cultural inclusion. To address these disparities, we need to formulate an overarching plan that addresses technology, political/policy reform, and teamwork internationally. This paper touched base on where the internet came from to where we currently stand and how we can remedy our current situation by acknowledging and addressing these issues. Addressing the differences of internet actress across the globe is indeed a complex problem that involves culture, politics/governance and socioeconomic barriers between developed and developing countries. This proposed solution focuses on how we can improve the global internet infrastructure, all while uphold ourselves to an ethical standard and build towards an equal future across the globe—through access to the internet. Moving forward, a global scope of teamwork is mandatory if we are to find success in a fair, open and inclusive internet.

References

American Library Association. (2024). *Net neutrality and open internet policies.* Retrieved from https://www.ala.org/advocacy/net-neutrality

Alvarez, C.-L., & Diez, J. M. S. (2023). The Content of the Right to Internet Access. Revista de Direito, Estado e Telecomunicacoes, 15(1), 31+. http://dx.doi.org.vlib.excelsior.edu/10.26512/lstr.v15i1.46859

Bradshaw, L. L. (2018). Using the Internet to create international experiences for students. *International Research and Review, 8*(1), 61-69. https://eric.ed.gov/?id=EJ1210916

Dao, M. (2017). Internet Use around the World: An Empirical Assessment. Perspectives on Global Development & Technology, 16(6),

683–699. https://doi.org/10.1163/15691497-12341456

Denver Public Library. (n.d.). *Udemy*. Denver Public Library. https://www.denverlibrary.org/udemy

Dorward, L. A. (2013). *Universal service funds and digital inclusion for all*. International Telecommunication Union. https://www.itu.int/en/ITU-D/Regulatory-Market/Documents/USF_final-en.pdf

Elon University. (n.d.). Imagining the internet's quick look at the early history of the internet. *Imagining the Internet*. Retrieved July 24, 2024, from https://www.elon.edu/u/imagining/time-capsule/early-90s/internet-history/

Federal Communications Commission. (2015). *Protecting and promoting the open internet*. Retrieved from https://www.fcc.gov/document/fact-sheet-protecting-and-promoting-open-internet

GIZ. (2020). Digital Inclusion: Bridging the Digital Divide in Africa. Retrieved from https://www.giz.de

Gnangnon, S. K. (2022). Internet, Participation in International Trade, and Tax Revenue Instability. *Journal of Economic Integration*, *37*(2), 267–315. http://vlib.excelsior.edu/login?url=https://search.ebscohost.com/login.aspx?direct=true&db=edsjsr&AN=edsjsr.27130222&site=eds-live&scope=site

Hoang, N. P., Niaki, A. A., Dalek, J., Knockel, J., Lin, P., Marczak, B., Crete-Nishihata, M., Gill, P., & Polychronakis, M. (2021). *How Great is the Great Firewall? Measuring China's DNS Censorship.* http://vlib.excelsior.edu/login?url=https://search.ebscohost.com/login.aspx?direct=true&db=edsarx&AN=edsarx.2106.02167&site=eds-live&scope=site

International Telecommunication Union. (2024). *Facts and figures: Focus on landlocked developing countries*. Retrieved from https://www.itu.int/itu-d/reports/statistics/facts-figures-for-lldc/

International Telecommunication Union. (2021). Internet for All: Connecting the Unconnected.

International Telecommunication Union. Retrieved from https://www.itu.int

International Telecommunication Union. (2000). *Regulatory approaches to facilitating the development of broadband infrastructure: Document 39*. International Telecommunication Union. https://www.itu.int/ITU-D/treg/Events/Seminars/GSR/DSR/documents/Document39.pdf

International Telecommunication Union. (2023). *The state of broadband: Broadband as a foundation for sustainable development*. International Telecommunication Union. https://www.itu.int/en/mediacentre/Pages/PR-2023-09-12-universal-and-meaningful-connectivity-by-2030.aspx

Jennings, L. M. (2005). Finding legal certainty for e-commerce: traditional personal jurisdiction analysis and the scope of the Zippo sliding scale. *Washburn Law Journal, 44*(2), 381–411. https://contentdm.washburnlaw.edu/digital/collection/wlj/id/5460/

Katikala, S. (2014). Google™ Project Loon. *InSight: Rivier Academic Journal, 10*(2), 1-6. Retrieved from https://www2.rivier.edu/journal/ROAJ-Fall-2014/J855-Katikala_Project-Loon.pdf

Kraemer, K. L., Dedrick, J., & Sharma, P. (2009). One laptop per child: Vision vs. reality. *Communications of the ACM, 52*(6), 66-73. https://doi.org/10.1145/1516046.1516063

Nieva, R. (2017, October 20). *Project Loon brings limited internet access to Puerto Rico.* CNET. https://www.cnet.com/tech/services-and-software/alphabet-google-project-loon-brings-limited-internet-access-to-puerto-rico/

Nothias, T. (2020). *Access granted: Facebook's free basics in Africa. Television & New Media, 42*(3). https://doi.org/10.1177/0163443719890530

Tiburcio, C., & Albuquerque, F. (2023). Territoriality, jurisdiction and internet: Some aspects of private international law/Territorialidade, jurisdição e internet: Alguns aspectos de direito internacional privado. *Revista Eletrônica de Direito Processual, 24*(3), 34+. https://link-gale-com.vlib.excelsior.edu/apps/doc/

A794678459/AONE?

u=ecvl&sid=ebsco&xid=9f61b247

UNESCO. (2023). Technology in education: A tool on whose terms? *Global Education Monitoring Report.* https://www.unesco.org/gem-report/en/technology

World Bank. (2024). *Public-private partnership data.* Retrieved July 23, 2024, from https://ppp.worldbank.org/public-private-partnership/tools/data

World Bank. (2024). *World Development Report 2024: Data and digital economy.* https://www.worldbank.org/en/publication/wdr2024

Zippo Manufacturing Co. v. Zippo Dot Com, Inc., 952 F. Supp. 1119 (W.D. Pa. 1997). https://law.justia.com/cases/federal/district-courts/FSupp/952/1119/1432344/#:~:text=When%20a%20defendant%20makes%20a,its%20services%20to%20Pennsylvania%20residents.

Appendix A: Case Studies

Case Study 1: The Impact of Internet Access in Rural Kenya

This case study explores how expanding internet access in rural Kenya has affected education, economic opportunities, and healthcare. The government's collaboration with private sector companies to install internet infrastructure in remote areas has led to improved access to online education platforms and telemedicine services, significantly benefiting local communities.

Case Study 2: Internet Censorship and Cultural Diversity in Iran

In Iran, internet censorship heavily impacts the free flow of information, affecting cultural expression and access to global knowledge. This case study examines how government controls on the internet intersect with cultural diversity, focusing on the challenges faced by minority groups in expressing their cultural identities online.

Case Study 3: MOOCs as a Tool for Education in Brazil

Massive Open Online Courses (MOOCs) have become a valuable resource for Brazilian students, especially those in underserved regions. This case study examines the role of platforms like Coursera and Khan Academy in providing accessible education and how these platforms help bridge the gap for students facing economic barriers.

Case Study 4: Digital Inclusion Initiatives in the European Union

The European Union's Digital Inclusion Strategy aims to ensure that all citizens, regardless of socio-economic status, have access to the internet and digital literacy programs. This case study analyzes the effectiveness of these initiatives in promoting social inclusion and reducing the digital divide across different member states.

Appendix B: Glossary of Terms

Digital Divide

The gap between individuals who have access to modern information and communication technology and those who do not.

MOOCs (Massive Open Online Courses)

Online courses aimed at unlimited participation and open access via the web. Platforms like Coursera, Udemy, and Khan Academy offer these courses, often at low or no cost.

ICT (Information and Communication Technology)

An umbrella term that includes any communication device or application, encompassing radio, television, cellular phones, computer and network hardware, satellite systems, and so on.

Internet Governance

The development and application of shared principles, norms, rules, decision-making procedures, and programs that shape the evolution and use of the internet.

Net Neutrality

The principle that all internet traffic should be treated equally, without discrimination or charging differently by user, content, website, platform, or application.

Open Internet

An internet where users can freely access and distribute information without restrictions, ensuring freedom of expression, privacy, and innovation.

Censorship

The suppression or prohibition of speech, communication, or information that is considered objectionable, harmful, sensitive, or inconvenient by governments, media outlets, or other controlling bodies.

Appendix C: Further Reading

Books

- "The Internet of Us: Knowing More and Understanding Less in the Age of Big Data" by Michael P. Lynch
  - Explores the implications of the digital age on knowledge and understanding, particularly in the context of the information overload brought on by the internet.
- "The Shallows: What the Internet Is Doing to Our Brains" by Nicholas Carr
  - Discusses how the internet changes the way we think, read, and remember, emphasizing the cognitive impacts of online engagement.
- "The Fourth Industrial Revolution" by Klaus Schwab

- Examines how the fusion of technologies is blurring the lines between the physical, digital, and biological spheres, and its impact on internet access and global communication.

Articles and Papers

- "Global Internet Access: Challenges and Opportunities" by Alvarez & Diez (2023)
    - A scholarly article that discusses the current state of global internet access, highlighting the disparities and potential solutions.
- "Internet Censorship and Its Global Implications" by Bradshaw (2018)
    - Explores the various methods of internet censorship employed by governments worldwide and their implications for global internet governance.

- "MOOCs and the Democratization of Education" by Hoang et al. (2021)
  - An analysis of how MOOCs have transformed access to education, particularly in economically disadvantaged regions.

Websites

- Internet Society (www.internetsociety.org)
  - A global organization that promotes the open development, evolution, and use of the internet for the benefit of all people throughout the world.
- Digital Divide Index (www.digitaldivideindex.org)
  - Provides data and insights on the digital divide in different regions, helping policymakers and researchers understand the scope of the issue.

- Coursera (www.coursera.org)
    - An online learning platform that offers courses from universities and companies around the world, contributing to the accessibility of education.

www.ingramcontent.com/pod-product-compliance
Lightning Source LLC
LaVergne TN
LVHW012247070526
838201LV00091B/149